The Library of Small Ecosystems ™

The Ecosystem of a Fallen Tree

Elaine Pascoe Photography by Dwight Kuhn

The Rosen Publishing Group's
PowerKids Press™
New York

Published in 2003 by The Rosen Publishing Group, Inc.
29 East 21st Street, New York, NY 10010

First Edition

Editor: Nancy MacDonell Smith
Book Design: Michael J. Caroleo

Photo Credits: Photos © Dwight Kuhn.

Pascoe, Elaine.
The ecosystem of a fallen tree / Elaine Pascoe ; photos by Dwight Kuhn.— 1st ed.
     p. cm. — (The library of small ecosystems)
Includes bibliographical references (p.   ).
Summary: Describes the plant and animal life associated with a fallen tree, all of which create a miniature, co-dependent ecosystem.
ISBN 0-8239-6308-X (lib. bdg.)
1. Animal ecology—Juvenile literature. 2. Trees—Ecology—Juvenile literature. 3. Dead trees—Juvenile literature. [1. Trees.
2. Habitat (Ecology) 3. Ecology.] I. Kuhn, Dwight, ill. II. Title.
QH541.5.F6 P36 2003
577—dc21

                                    2001007768

Manufactured in the United States of America

Contents

A Fallen Tree

A fallen tree lies on the ground. The tree is dead. There is still life in it, though. How can that be? After a tree dies, it becomes a home for many different living things. Animals take shelter underneath it. Insects tunnel into the wood. **Fungi** and moss grow on the trunk.

The tree and the plants and animals that use it are all members of a small **ecosystem**. An ecosystem is a community of living and nonliving things. The members of this little community depend on one another. Each one has its own role in the ecosystem.

This fallen tree is covered with a soft coating of moss. Moss helps to break down the wood of a fallen tree. This process brings nutrients to the soil.

From Tree to Soil

As it lies on the ground, a fallen tree slowly changes. Its wood rots, or decomposes. This means the wood breaks down into simple parts and crumbles away, forming new soil. This process takes many years, and it does not happen by itself. Insects **bore** into the wood. Tiny **bacteria** feed on the wood, helping to break it down. Fungi that live on a fallen tree help to break down the wood, too.

When it was alive, the tree took in **nutrients** from the soil. It used the nutrients to grow. When the tree dies and decomposes, the nutrients return to the soil.

This tree has been dead for seven years. Inset: This is the same tree, 13 years later. A new tree is growing from the old one.

The eastern box turtle spends the winter in a deep sleep under a fallen tree. The box turtle feeds on worms, slugs, and snails, which can be found at a fallen tree.

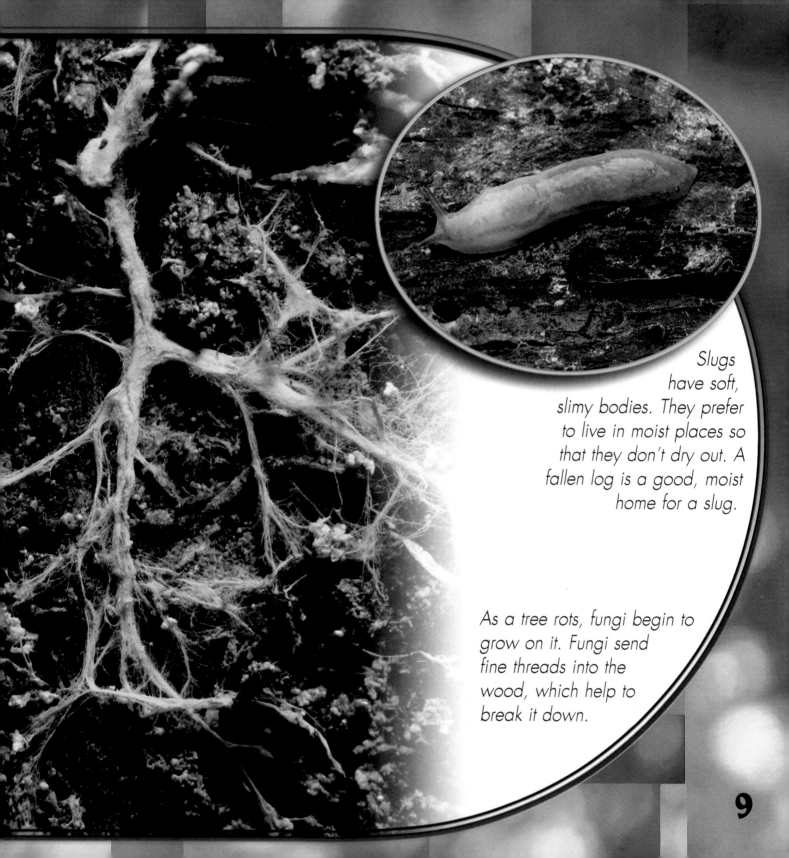

Slugs have soft, slimy bodies. They prefer to live in moist places so that they don't dry out. A fallen log is a good, moist home for a slug.

As a tree rots, fungi begin to grow on it. Fungi send fine threads into the wood, which help to break it down.

A Home for Mice

A nest under a fallen tree is a good place for mice to raise their young. A little white-footed mouse can make a nest there and line it with soft grass. When her babies are born, they are blind and have no fur. The mother feeds them with milk produced by her body, and the young mice grow quickly. In about 10 days, they have fur. A few days later, their eyes open. Then they are ready to begin exploring the area around their home, looking for seeds and other things to eat. When the young mice are about three weeks old, they are ready to leave the shelter of their nest under the tree trunk.

These baby mice are three days old. Top Inset: *The white-footed mouse uses a fallen tree as a place to raise her young.* Bottom Inset: *By the time the mice are 13 days old, they have fur.*

Visitors and House Hunters

Before it rots away, a fallen tree gives shelter to many kinds of animals. Skunks or bobcats may make homes in its trunk. Chipmunks may dig holes called burrows under the trunk. Chipmunks collect acorns and other nuts and store them in these burrows. Burrows are where chipmunks spend the winter hibernating, or in a deep sleep. Every so often, they wake up for an acorn snack.

Weasels may come to **explore** a fallen tree. Weasels are predators. Predators are animals that kill and eat other animals. Weasels hunt for mice and other small animals that may be living in or under a fallen tree. For weasels, a fallen tree is a good place to find food.

Chipmunks gather acorns to eat during the winter. Inset: Weasels are carnivores, which means that they eat meat.

The skunk is a member of the weasel family. Skunks are always black-and-white.

This bobcat cub lives in a hollow in a fallen tree. Bobcats have large paws and short bodies.

At five weeks of age, a white-footed mouse is not yet fully grown, but it can take care of itself.

15

Turtles and More

Amphibians and reptiles also find shelter in a fallen tree. The salamander is an amphibian. Its skin dries out easily, but the log's rotting wood is damp and helps to keep the animal moist.

For the box turtle, a fallen tree may be a winter home. The turtle is a reptile. In the fall, the turtle digs down under the log. Then it pulls its head and feet inside its shell and hibernates until spring.

Green snakes are also reptiles. They come to a fallen tree to hunt for insects, which they eat. The female green snake may lay her eggs under the log. The dampness will keep the eggs from drying out. The snake does not stay to care for them. When they hatch, the young snakes will hunt for food on their own.

Top: *The turtle's hard shell protects its soft body.* Bottom: *A salamander leaves the fallen tree at night to look for food.*

Sow Bugs, Slugs, and Spiders

Some other animals find the dampness of the rotting log just right, too. Among them are slugs, sow bugs, and **millipedes**. Slugs are related to snails, but slugs do not have shells. Sow bugs and millipedes look like insects, but they belong to different animal families. Sow bugs are related to lobsters! Besides finding dampness, many of these animals find food at the log. They eat bits of dead leaves and other dead material. By doing this, they help the tree to decompose.

Spiders find food at a fallen tree, too. The wolf spider hunts for smaller animals to eat, such as a sow bug or a millipede. The female wolf spider carries her silk egg case with her as she hunts. When the eggs hatch, the baby spiders ride on their mother's back for about a week. Then they are ready to live on their own.

Wolf spiders carry their young with them until the young are ready to hunt alone. Inset: Sow bugs have plates that protect them like a suit of armor.

A smooth green snake can grow to be about 20 inches (51 cm) long. A fallen tree is both a hunting ground and a nursery for the smooth green snake.

This baby smooth green snake is hatching from its egg, which has been under a fallen tree. Snake eggs are soft and leathery, not hard-shelled like birds' eggs.

A millipede can have up to 355 pairs of legs! Millipedes can be anywhere from less than $\frac{1}{10}$ inch to 11 inches (.25–28 cm) long.

21

New Plants

As a fallen tree rots, plants begin to grow on it. Mosses usually grow first. These small plants form a soft, green mat on the log. They help to hold dampness in the wood, and the dampness makes the log a good place for other plants to grow. In time larger plants, such as ferns, may take root there and start to grow. Wildflowers and even new trees may **sprout** from seeds that land on a fallen tree.

These new plants send roots down into the soft, rotting wood. The roots soak up nutrients from the log, so the new plants can grow. The roots also break the wood apart, helping the fallen tree to decompose.

This moss has sent up shoots. The shoots let out spores. Spores are special cells that can grow into new living things. Inset: *Ferns grow best in damp places.*

Tunnel Makers

A rotting tree is a home for beetles, termites, and other insects that tunnel into the wood. As they chew through the wood, they help to break down the log.

Termites eat wood. Carpenter ants chew away the wood, but they do not eat it. They hollow out tunnels and rooms for their nests inside the log. Members of a carpenter ant colony have different jobs. Some make tunnels. Some hunt for food. Some tend the eggs laid by the colony's queen. Others look after the **larvae** that hatch from the eggs. The larvae grow until they are about ¼ inch (.6 cm) long, nearly the size of adults. Then each larva spins a cocoon around itself. The cocoon is made of silk that the ant larvae make using special body parts. Inside its cocoon, a larva **pupates**, or changes into an adult.

Termites live in groups called colonies. Their nests may be in the log or in the ground. Inset: It takes about three weeks for ant larvae to turn into adults.

Eyed click beetles often live either in or under fallen trees. This beetle is named for its spots, which look like eyes, and for the noise it makes. If an eyed click beetle is put on its back, it will flip over with a loud click.

Carpenter ant larvae look like fat, white worms. The larvae pupate, or change into adults, inside silk cocoons.

27

Speeding Up Decay

A damp, rotting tree is a good place for mushrooms and other fungi to grow. Mushrooms are food for mice and other animals. A mushroom is only part of a fungus, though. The rest is made up of tiny, white threads called **hyphae**. They grow down into the log like roots. The hyphae produce chemicals that break down the wood, so the fungus can soak up nutrients.

Lichens and **slime molds** break down the wood in much the same way. Lichens are made up of two different kinds of living things, fungi and **single-celled organisms** called **algae**. A slime mold is a single-celled organism that creeps across a rotting log, eating bacteria and dead material. Lichens and slime molds speed up decay, as do fungi.

Top: *Slime molds grow best in moist places.* Bottom: *Lichens, such as this Turk's cap lichen, grow very slowly. A new lichen grows when part of an existing lichen breaks off and begins to grow elsewhere on a fallen tree.* Inset: *A bracket fungus grows in the rotting wood.*

29

A Fallen-Tree Community

A fallen tree is the center of a little community whose members all depend on one another. A fallen tree provides shelter for many animals, from skunks to sow bugs. It provides food for plants, bacteria, fungi, and insects, such as termites. Many of those living things in turn become food for larger animals.

A fallen tree community also plays an important role in a larger community, the ecosystem of a forest. The living things that feed on the tree take the nutrients they need but leave other nutrients. Those nutrients return to the soil as the dead tree decomposes. In the soil, they help new plants to grow.

Glossary

algae (AL-jee) Simple living things that can make their own food.

amphibians (am-FIH-bee-unz) A group of animals that spend the first part of their lives in water and the rest on land.

bacteria (bak-TEER-ee-uh) Simple single-celled organisms, so small that they can only be seen with a microscope.

bore (BOHR) To make a hole by digging or pushing.

ecosystem (EE-koh-sis-tem) A community of living things and the surroundings, such as air, soil, and water, in which they live.

explore (ik-SPLOR) To go over carefully or examine.

fungi (FUN-jeye) Members of a family of living things that includes mushrooms.

hyphae (HY-fee) Fine threads that make up most kinds of fungi.

larvae (LAR-vee) The plural form of larva. The early life stage of certain animals that differs greatly from the adult stage.

lichens (LY-kenz) Living partnerships of algae and fungi.

millipedes (MIH-lih-peedz) Small animals with long, thin bodies and anywhere from 9 to 355 pairs of legs.

nutrients (NOO-tree-ints) Anything that a living thing needs to live and grow.

pupates (PYOO-paytz) Changes from a larva to an adult.

reptiles (REP-tylz) Cold-blooded animals that hatch from eggs, such as crocodiles and snakes.

single-celled organisms (SING-gul-seld OR-guh-nih-zumz) Living things whose bodies are made up of just one unit, or cell.

slime molds (SLYM MOLDZ) Simple living things that live in damp places and help to break down dead plant and animal materials.

sprout (SPROWT) Begin to grow.

Index

B
bacteria, 6, 29, 30

C
carpenter ants, 24
cocoon, 24

D
decompose(s), 6, 18,
    23, 30

E
ecosystem, 5, 30
eggs, 17, 18, 24

F
fungi, 5, 29–30

L
larva(e), 24
lichens, 29

M
mice, 11–12, 29
millipedes, 18
mosses, 23

N
nest(s), 11, 24
nutrients, 6, 23,
    29–30

P
predators, 12
pupates, 24

S
salamander, 17
shelter, 11–12, 17, 30
snake(s), 17
sow bugs, 18, 30

Web Sites

Due to the changing nature of Internet links, PowerKids Press has developed an online list of Web sites related to the subject of this book. This site is updated regularly. Please use this link to access the list:
www.powerkidslinks.com/lse/ftreeeco/